Introduction

This book is for anyone who has had a (lovey) Stuffed animal that made a difference in your life. I know mine is still with me and will be with me until I die. He is a 6 inch Cheetah and his name is Tiger, and he has been my best friend since I was 7 years old.

How my Tiger and I met.

One day I was at the store, looking in the toy section, when I saw him. he spoke to me. No reason at all, he wasn't ornate, extra furry, brightly colored or any more special than the animals next to him, but to me it was love at first sign and I know I had to have him. After begging, pleading and as seven year olds do, whining with real tears, my parents finally gave in.

Our Loveys

Special Thanks

To my loving husband for the endless encouragement

To my mother for helping me edit,proof read and have inspiration.

To my sister for her forever dedication to her blackie.

To my aunt who also had a big role in inspiration for the pictures
(Green and Blue all the way!)

And to my children who were my reason for creating this special book!

Thank you so much, I love you all!

5 Truths About Your Lovey

#1

Bad Dream
HERO

Throughout the night,
Your lovey will fight.
Bad dreams and fears,
Throughout the years.

From dusk till dawn,
Through years and on.
Your lovey will fight,
Till morning light.

#2

Band-Aid Buddy

By your side,
Whenever you need.
From needles that prick,
To owies that bleed.

Always near you,
In a hospital bed.
With casts on your feet,
Or no hair on your head.

#3

THE TEAR CATCHER

Upon their fur, you can cry.
They soak up pain, and never lie.
If you lost someone,
Or just feeling blue.
Don't worry they will be there,
Right next to you.

Whether hurt by a fall,
Or stung by a bee.
They whisper so sweetly,
"You'll Always have me."

#4

THE

KNIGHT
LIGHT

Loveys will be there,
When you are asleep.
Fighting under the bed,
With the monsters
Tickling your feet!

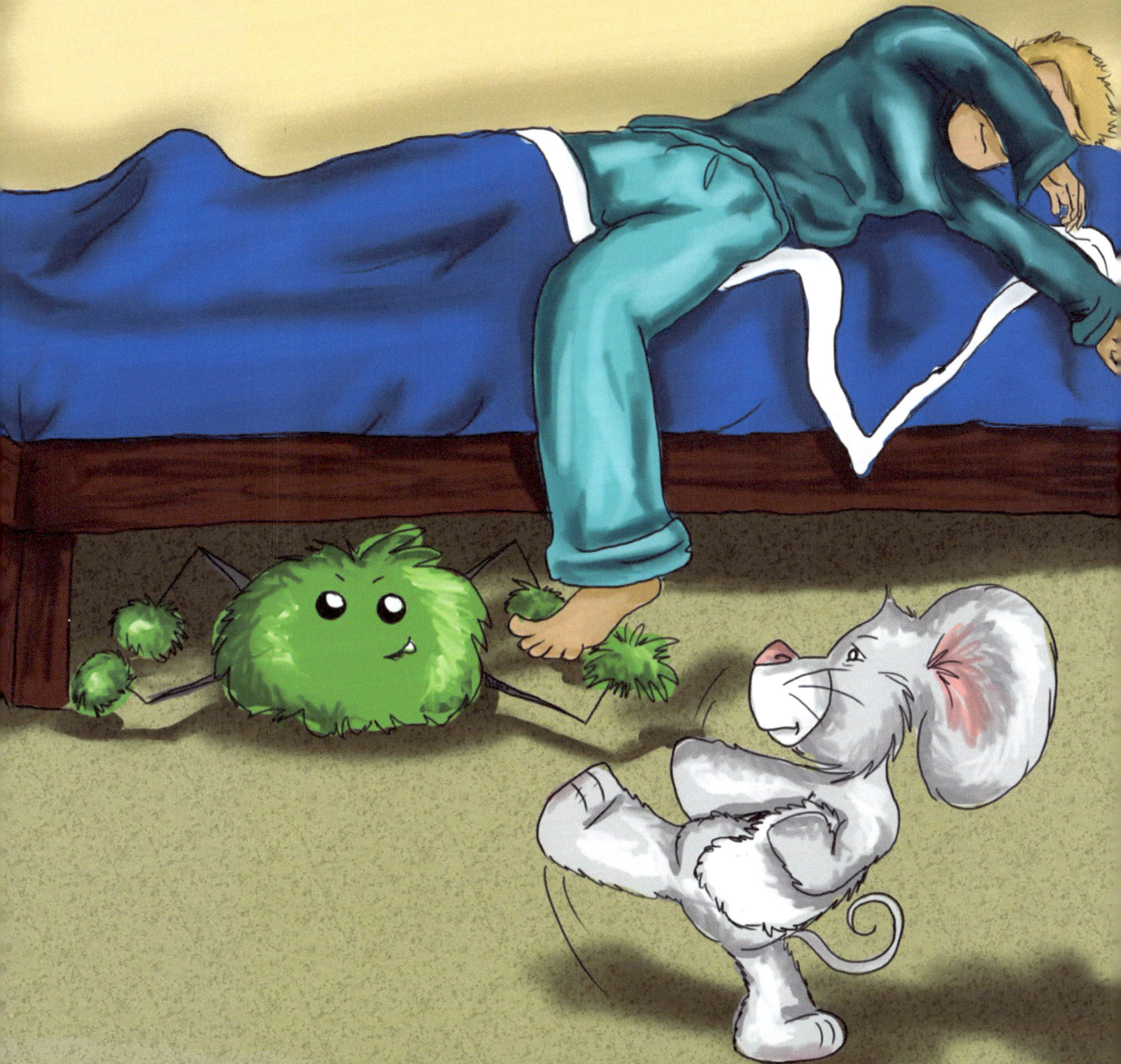

If there are noises in the closet,
Or winds that are loud.
Loveys will guard you,
And keep you safe and sound.

#5

Forever Yours

Lovey's will be there,
When you have grown tall.
Whether in your dreams,
or just down the hall.

Your parents have a secret,
Just ask them what they do.
When they are scared and lonely,
Guess what?
Mom and Dad need loveys too!

The End

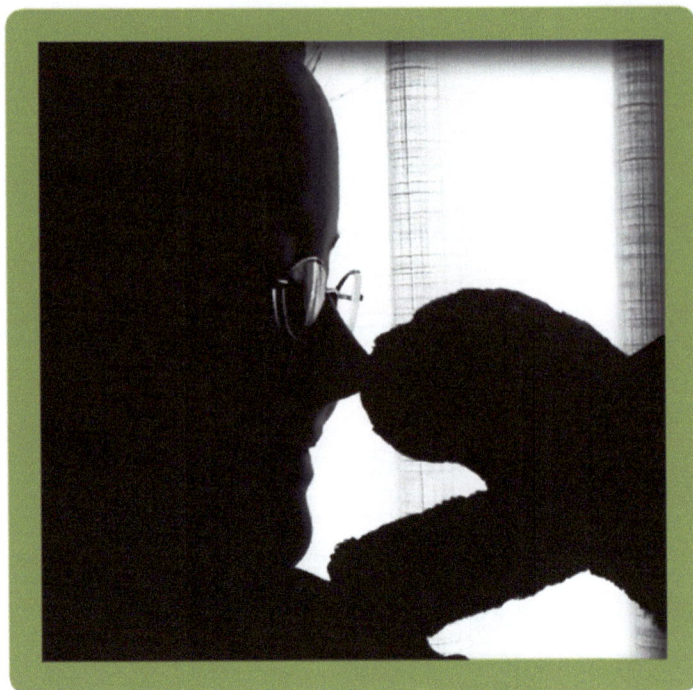

This is for all of you who remember their lovey,
best friend, boo, or blankie.

To: Tiger, Blackie, Racky, Ducky,
Blankie, and Tom Tinker

Without all of you there would be no book!

www.ingramcontent.com/pod-product-compliance
Lightning Source LLC
Chambersburg PA
CBHW042120040426
42449CB00003B/128